James Cook

Discover The Life Of An Explorer

Trish Kline

Rourke
Publishing LLC
Vero Beach, Florida 32964

www.rourkepublishing.com

PHOTO CREDITS: IRC-www.historypictures.com: cover, pages 4, 10, 12; ©Hulton/Archive by Getty images: pages 7, 13, 17, 21; © James P. Rowan: pages 15, 18; © Painet. Inc.: title page; © PhotoDisc: page 8.

Title page: A replica of the *Endeavour*—one of Captain James Cook's ships

Editor: Frank Sloan

Cover design by Nicola Stratford

Library of Congress Cataloging-in-Publication Data

Kline, Trish
    James Cook / Trish Kline.
        p. cm. — (Discover the life of an explorer)
    Summary: Introduces the life of James Cook, the English explorer and mapmaker who sailed to many lands and claimed them for England, including what are now New Zealand, Australia, and the Hawaiian Islands.
     Includes bibliographical references and index.
    ISBN 1-58952-292-3
    1. Cook, James, 1728-1779—Juvenile literature. 2. Explorers—Great Britain—Biography—Juvenile literature. 3. Voyages around the world—Juvenile literature. [1. Cook, James, 1728-1779. 2. Explorers. 3. Voyages around the world.] I. Title

G420.C65 K65 2002
910'.92—dc21   2002017041

Printed in the USA

CG/CG

TABLE OF CONTENTS

FROM DECKHAND TO MAPMAKER

James Cook was born October 27, 1728, in England. At 18, he went to sea. He was a **deckhand** on a ship that carried coal. At 27, he joined England's navy.

Cook was a good **navigator.** He was also a very good **mapmaker.** Cook was sent to Canada to draw maps about the waters of the St. Lawrence River.

FIRST VOYAGE

Cook led his first **voyage** in 1769. He sailed to many new lands. He claimed these lands for England. These new lands were the present-day countries of New Zealand and Australia. These discoveries helped England to build a great **empire.**

James Cook and his crew raised the English flag in Australia.

MILES AND MILES OF ICE

Soon, Cook was sent on a second voyage. He sailed south. He sailed farther south than anyone had before him. He wanted to learn if there was land on the most southern part of the world.

Cook sailed all the way to present-day Antarctica. However, huge **icebergs** kept Cook from finding land. All he could see were miles and miles of ice. Cook never knew how close to land he had sailed.

Icebergs kept Cook from reaching land in Antarctica.

DISCOVERING THE HAWAIIAN ISLANDS

Cook returned to England. The navy made him a captain. In 1776, Cook set out on his third voyage. He wanted to find a sea route between Europe and Asia. He sailed for two years. As he sailed across the Pacific Ocean, Cook discovered the Hawaiian Islands.

Natives greeted Cook when he landed in Hawaii.

Natives offered gifts to Cook.

The ship Discovery took Cook on his final voyage.

SAILING THE PACIFIC

Cook set sail again. He sailed east. Soon, he again saw land. This land was the present-day west coast of the United States. Cook sailed north along the coast. He sailed all the way to the Arctic Ocean.

There were great walls of ice everywhere. Cook could not **navigate** his ship around the icebergs. He decided to sail back to the warm **climate** of the Hawaiian Islands.

Captain Cook sailed along the Pacific northwest on his third voyage.

KILLED BY NATIVES

Back at the islands, natives stole some supplies from Cook's ship. Cook and his soldiers went to find their supplies. Cook took the king as a captive. He said he would set the king free when the supplies were returned.

Cook returned to Hawaii in 1779. He was killed during a fight with natives.

The natives were not happy. They waited for Cook on the beach. A fight broke out. The natives beat Cook with clubs. Then, they stabbed him with their spears.

Cook died from his wounds. His ship sailed out to sea. Cook's body was dropped over the side of the ship. It was February 22, 1779. Cook was almost 51 years old.

A statue in London, England, honors the discoveries of James Cook.

AROUND THE WORLD

James Cook was a great navigator and mapmaker. His exploration led to many colonies across the Pacific Ocean. His discoveries claimed many lands for the great empire of England.

James Cook sailed around the world. He also sailed the oceans nearest the North and South poles.

Cook kept a journal of many of his voyages.

... after two hours calm, in the Latitude of 39...

... the Wind at West, the next day it fixed at N...

... increased to a fresh gale, with which we steered di...

... Lizard and on

... made the Land about Plymouth, Maker Church

... o'clock in the After-noon, bore N. 10. W. distan...

... ques; this bearing and distance, shew'd that...

... of Mr. Kendal's Watch, in Longitude was only...

... was too far to the West ——

James Cook

IMPORTANT DATES TO REMEMBER

1728	Born in England
1746	Went to sea as a deckhand
1769	Led his first voyage
1776	Discovered the Hawaiian Islands
1779	Stabbed to death and buried at sea

GLOSSARY

climate (KLY mit) — average weather at a place over many years

deckhand (DEK hand) — person on a ship who works on the deck

empire (EM pyre) — a large kingdom or nation

icebergs (ICE burgs) — large pieces of ice that break away from larger moving bodies of ice

mapmaker (MAP mayker) — a person who creates maps

navigate (NAV i gayt) — to steer the way you want to go

navigator (NAV i gayt er) — one who guides or pilots, such as captain of a ship

voyage (VOY ij) — a trip to a faraway place

INDEX

Further Reading

Middleton, Haydn. *Captain Cook: The Great Ocean Explorer.* Oxford University Press, 1998.

Shields, Charles J. *James Cook and the Exploration of the Pacific.* Chelsea House Publishing, 2001.

Websites To Visit

http://www.pbs.org

http://www.mariner.org   (The Mariner's Museum, Newport News, VA)

http://www.nmm.ac.uk   (The National Maritime Museum, London, England)

About The Author

Trish Kline has written a great number of nonfiction books for the school and library market. Her publishing credits include two dozen books, as well as hundreds of newspaper and magazine articles, anthologies, short stories, poetry, and plays. She lives in Helena, Montana.